PATHWAY [barcode sticker] ES

CW01582635

Fear and Freedom

MATTHEW 8-12

BY PETER COLLIER

matthiasmedia

Fear and Freedom
Pathway Bible Guides: Matthew 8-12

Matthias Media
(St Matthias Press Ltd. ACN 067 558 365)
PO Box 225
Kingsford NSW 2032
Australia
Telephone: (02) 9663 1478; international: +61-2-9663-1478
Facsimile: (02) 9663 3265; international: +61-2-9663-3265
Email: info@matthiasmedia.com.au
Internet: www.matthiasmedia.com.au

Matthias Media (USA)
Telephone: 724 964 8152; international: +1-724-964-8152
Facsimile: 724 964 8166; international: +1-724-964-8166
Email: sales@matthiasmedia.com
Internet: www.matthiasmedia.com

ISBN 978 1 921441 32 5

Cover design and typesetting by Lankshear Design Pty Ltd.

CONTENTS

BEFORE YOU BEGIN

A good way to get to know the true character of someone famous is to find out more about their early years. Seeing what people were like before they became famous reveals a great deal about their true identity. It is exciting, too, going back to where everything began for them. You are transported back to the early days, recognizing the greatness that one day others will also see.

This is true in the case of Jesus.

Looking at the early days of Jesus' ministry gives us a sense of what lies ahead for him, and gives us a powerful insight into his character and appeal. This early glimpse is what we find in Matthew 8-12. These chapters provide us with an authentic opportunity to get to know Jesus and to understand who he is, what he did and what he demands of his followers. In these chapters, we see Jesus' fearsome authority and his tender compassion. We see him living up to the extraordinary Old Testament expectations, all based on God's promises about the coming Messiah. We see opposition beginning and hardening against him, and we witness his courageous response. We see his faultless integrity and hear him teaching his disciples. In short: we meet the real Jesus in his early ministry in a biography he authorized.

The other thing we find in Matthew 8-12 is a vast array of different responses to Jesus. He is loved, hated, feared, labelled, pleaded with, questioned. People leave their jobs because of him; people stake their reputations on opposing him. No-one can sit on the fence. This examination of Jesus' early years is confronting for us too, for Jesus always demands a response. A right fear of Jesus' power and authority will lead, paradoxically, to true freedom.

It is my prayer that your examination of Jesus in these chapters will be genuine, and that your response to Jesus will be worthy of him.

Peter Collier
October 2008

1. JESUS: BEFORE HE WAS FAMOUS

Matthew 7:28-8:27

Getting started

When someone says of a celebrity, "I knew them before they were famous", it immediately arouses our curiosity. Why do we like to know what famous people were like before they achieved their fame?

Light from the Word

Read Matthew 7:28-8:27.

1. In Matthew 5-7, Jesus has just given his most famous speech, known as the 'Sermon on the Mount'. After finishing this, "the crowds were astonished at his teaching, for he was teaching them as one who had authority ..." (7:28-29).

    a. What evidence is there in this passage of the *authority* of Jesus' words?

    Actions
    Healings

    b. How far over creation does Jesus' authority extend?

    Distance
    Many people
    Harsh Word
    Said some harsh things

2. Later, in Matthew 9:35-36, we will read a summary that includes the statement, "When [Jesus] saw the crowds, he had compassion for them, because they were harassed and helpless, like sheep without a shepherd".

    a. What evidence is there, in our present passage, of Jesus' *compassion*?

    Centurion under different religious system
    8 v 17
    Peter's mum
    was consequently

    He uses his authority in compassion

b. What reason is given in the passage for why Jesus is acting in this way? (Note especially 8:17. If you have time, you may like to compare Isaiah 52:13-53:12, which is where this quote comes from.)

3. The disciples marvel at Jesus in 8:27.

a. Why did Jesus marvel (8:10)?

b. Why does Jesus seem surprised (8:26)?

4. "... but the Son of Man has nowhere to lay his head" (8:20).

a. Why is this surprising?

b. What attitude, then, should Jesus' disciples have to where they 'lay their heads' (that is, where they live)?

5. "Follow me, and leave the dead to bury their own dead" (8:22).

a. What does this command tell us about Jesus?

WHAT DOES THIS MEAN TOM

b. What ~~relationships~~ things do you have that may challenge Jesus for 'top spot'? What should you do about this?

To do lists.

6. What else do we learn in the rest of this section about what it means to follow Jesus? (See, for example, 8:8-13 and 8:26.)

To finish

The disciples ask the question in 8:27, "What sort of man is this …?"

- How would your workmates or friends answer this question?

- What sort of man would you say Jesus was before he was famous?

- Given your answer, how should you act?

Give thanks and pray

- Give thanks for the fact that Jesus' authority is matched by his compassion.
- Pray that you would have faith in Jesus and be prepared to give priority to following him ahead of anyone else.
- Pray that our fear of what we might lose, in worldly terms, will not stop us from embracing the freedom Jesus offers.

2. JESUS: DOCTOR TO SINNERS

Matthew 8:28-9:36

Getting started

Which people does our society regard as being morally sick? What cures are offered for their ills?

Light from the Word

Read Matthew 8:28-9:36.

1. What evidence is there in this passage of:

   a. the *authority* of Jesus?

   Answers v14-15
   Extent of miracles

   b. the *compassion* of Jesus?

   All diseases
   No bias (heals all sorts)
   goes to the unlovely (tax collectors, blind men ...)

2. There are a number of responses to Jesus' authority in this passage.

   a. Among the negative responses, what evidence is there of growing opposition?

   v34 → unsure, fearful
   v3, v11 → Don't agree with him
   v31 → don't obey

   b. What underlies this opposition?

   Doubt + Confusion (v33)
   fear
   Religious misunderstanding

   c. What does a 'good' response to Jesus' authority look like?

   Amazement 9 33
   9 21 Reached out to him in desperation
   9 8 Praised God

3. The people of the Gadarenes met Jesus and begged him to leave their region (8:34).

   a. What is wrong with their response?

   b. How do people today respond in a similar way?

Turn back to the Old Testament and read Ezekiel 34:1-6.

4. What were the 'shepherds' of Israel doing?

Read Ezekiel 34:11-16.

5. What did God say he would do?

Go back to Matthew 8:28-9:36.

6. How does Jesus' action fulfil Ezekiel's prophecy?

7. Our passage has highlighted a number of responses to Jesus, good and bad. What do these responses tell us about the character of those responding?

To finish

- Do you think Jesus had come to call the Pharisees? Why or why not?

- What warnings can we take away from the Pharisees in particular?

Give thanks and pray

- Thank God for keeping his promise to send the good shepherd, Jesus.
- Pray that we would see our need for 'Dr Jesus'. Pray for one friend who does not see their need for Jesus—that they *would* see it.

3. JESUS: LORD OF THE HARVEST

Matthew 9:35-10:23

Getting started

When embarking on a project, why is it important to have right expectations? Can you think of examples where having wrong expectations had very negative effects?

Light from the Word

Read Matthew 9:35-10:23.

1. What evidence is there in this passage of Jesus' authority?

Does healing

but does verbal handover with disciples...

2. What task does Jesus give the disciples?

Harvest amongst Jews?

3. What suggests that this task is urgent?

Cautionary lines

time frame: Son of Man comes,

4. What does the task Jesus gives the disciples have to do with the events described in Matthew 9:35-37?

Prayer for the work of 10:1-23 /

Not enough to do the task of

speaking truth...

5. If we wish to see more people 'harvested' for Jesus, what ought we to do?

Genuine friendship

6. How are the disciples to go about their task?

Freely you have recieved, freely you give

Wise + innocent (scared)

7. What warnings does Jesus give the disciples?

Hated
Flogging(s) / death
family disputes

8. Jesus is clearly speaking to the disciples about a specific task.

a. What is specific about the task? (Compare with Matthew 28:18-20 and Luke 22:35-36.)

Different group of people
Message fleshed out
Jesus is with them.

b. What aspects of the task are common to all Christian ministry?

Speaking "Go + tell"

9. According to Matthew 10:17-23, what does it mean to be "wise as serpents"?

Wary of humanity...

10. "... you will be hated by all for my name's sake" (10:22). Why, then, follow Jesus?

Because we're lost sheep

V22 → He who stands...

To finish

What expectations ought 'workers' in the Lord's harvest field have, according to this passage?

I'm not literally being Mashed up..

Give thanks and pray

- Give thanks for those who brought the good news of the kingdom of heaven to you.
- Ask the Lord of the harvest to send out workers into the harvest field where you are. Pray for a plentiful harvest and for innocence, shrewdness and courage for Jesus' workers.

4. JESUS: THE ONE TO FEAR

Matthew 10:24-42

Getting started

What makes you afraid? How do you overcome that fear?

Being lonely
Illness
Helplessness
Thunder
Crime
Unknown

Rationalise them
Distraction

Light from the Word

Read Matthew 10:24-42.

1. What does Jesus teach his disciples to expect?

2. What do these verses show about Jesus' opinion of himself?

3. In our last study, we saw that in the first part of this speech (10:5-23), Jesus was giving the disciples a specific task, and that several things he said applied only to their particular situation. Which parts (if any) of what Jesus says in our current passage apply *only* to the twelve disciples?

4. Who does Jesus mean by "them" and "those" in verses 26 and 28?

5. Why are the disciples not to be afraid of "them"?

v31

6. What might fear of "them" stop the disciples doing?

proclamation [illegible] ...

7. Who is the equivalent of "them" for you?

Could be anyone

8. What might fear of "them" prevent us from doing?

living in an obviously faithful life
Proclamation

9. What should we do instead?

Being afraid

10. What might loving our family (or our life!) more than Jesus look like in practice?

I dont know!

11. What is the significance of Jesus saying "for my sake" (v. 39) and "because he is a disciple" (v. 42)?

To finish

Who are some 'disciples of Jesus' you could receive? How could you receive them?

Give thanks and pray

- Give thanks for Jesus' promise to stand by those who stand by him.
- Thank God that *true* fear of Jesus will result in freedom from fear.
- Pray for:
  - courage to acknowledge Jesus before people
  - willingness to lose our lives for his sake
  - strength to stand by his messengers and disciples.

5. JESUS: DON'T LOOK FOR ANOTHER

Matthew 11:1-19

Getting started

Think of a friend who has doubts about Jesus. What doubts do they have? How would you go about answering them?

Light from the Word

Read Matthew 3:11-12.

1. What was John the Baptist expecting?

More power/way better than JtB
Holy Spirit + fire
Winnowing / judgment

Extreme character

Read Matthew 11:1-19.

2. John's disciples ask if Jesus is "the one who is to come" (v. 3).

    a. Why might they have done this?

    b. What is Jesus' answer? (See verses 4-6. Jesus' answer refers to Isaiah 61:1 and Isaiah 35:3-6, so compare these passages.)

    c. How does Jesus' answer help us with our own doubts?

3. What do we learn here about John the Baptist?

4. Read Malachi 3:1 and 4:5-6. (In the Bible, Malachi is the book before Matthew!) What will happen after the 'messenger' and 'Elijah' come?

    - Malachi 3:1

    - Malachi 4:5-6

5. If John the Baptist is the 'messenger' and the 'Elijah', then who is Jesus?

One to come

6. Jesus says, "He who has ears to hear, let him hear" (v. 15). What is he commanding us to hear (vv. 4-15)?

Summary → Follow him!

Read Matthew 11:16-19.

7. How did Jesus' generation respond to him and to John the Baptist?

8. How does *our* generation respond?

To finish

If a Christian friend began to have doubts about Jesus because of hardship (like John the Baptist), how could you use this passage to encourage them?

Give thanks and pray

- Give thanks to God for keeping his promise about sending a messenger like Elijah in the person of John the Baptist.
- Pray we would be prepared to listen and receive what Jesus teaches about himself.
- Pray for anyone you know who may be struggling with doubts, that they would not 'take offence' at Jesus.

6. JESUS: THE WAY TO FIND REST

Matthew 11:20-30

Getting started

Which of the following do you think would be the most popular recommendations for getting peace of mind?

- ○ Take a holiday
- ○ Play or watch some sport
- ○ Be told how to live your life
- ○ Have a coffee with friends
- ○ Spend time with family
- ○ Hear about God's judgement
- ○ Go shopping
- ○ Take a long walk outdoors

Light from the Word

Read Matthew 11:20-24.

1. What do we learn about the cities of Chorazin, Bethsaida and Capernaum?

Miracles happened there
unrepentant.

Tyre, Sidon and Sodom were cities that had been judged severely in the Old Testament because of great wickedness. Yet Jesus says it will be more bearable on the day of judgement for these cities than for Chorazin, Bethsaida and Capernaum.

2. Why does Jesus denounce these cities so strongly? What had they done that was so wrong?

unrepentance

3. What warning is there for those people who know more about Jesus' ministry and teaching than others?

Read Matthew 11:25-30.

4. What does Jesus say here about:

   a. God the Father?

   Only he knows the Son v27
   Lord of heaven + earth
   Wisdom + learned hidden, children revealed to
   No one knows Son except father

   b. himself?

   No one knows him except father
   all things given to him
   offers rest
   gentle + humble
   yoke → easy
   Son chooses to reveal father to people

   c. people?

   Can be brought to the father through the Son.
   Can have rest.
   Weary people.

5. Given what Jesus says here, how would you respond to the person who insists, "We can't know what God is like"?

Jesus can reveal the father
He is knowable.

6. What command does Jesus give in this section?

Come to me,

7. To whom does he give this command?

weary + burdened

8. What does he promise to those who obey?

Rest

What is the connection back to the father/son/reveal vs??

9. What happens if we disobey Jesus' command here?

10. How does Jesus' way of finding 'rest for our souls' differ from the ways recommended in our society?

To finish

Why are we sometimes reluctant to come to Jesus, take his yoke upon ourselves and learn from him? How do the things Jesus says in this passage help us overcome this reluctance?

Wanting to be in control.
Hard truths, accepting help.
See it as "extra", "burden".

Give thanks and pray

- Thank God the Father that we can know him through his Son Jesus.
- Give thanks for the fact that Jesus is a humble and gentle master, and for the rest and freedom he gives for our souls.
- Pray that we would be prepared to take Jesus' yoke upon ourselves, and not be stubborn and refuse to learn from him.
- Pray for a friend or family member who has not yet found rest for their souls in Jesus, that they would come to him.

Rest

7. JESUS: THE LORD OF REST

Matthew 11:28-12:21

Getting started

"If you lose sight of the Big Picture, you will make mistakes with the details." What do you think? What examples can you give to support your view?

Light from the Word

Read Matthew 11:28-12:21. (Note: the Hebrew word 'sabbath' means 'rest'.)

1. Jesus speaks of his 'yoke' in Matthew 11:28-30.

   a. What does Jesus say he and his yoke are like?

   b. What evidence is there of this in Matthew 12:1-21?

   c. How does this contrast with the Pharisees and their yoke, as seen here?

2. What else do we learn about Jesus in Matthew 12:1-21?

3. Why does Jesus say the disciples are innocent?

4. Why, then, do the Pharisees say the disciples are doing what is unlawful? What have they failed to see?

5. In what ways could we make the same mistake as the Pharisees?

6. Jesus performs an astonishing miracle in this passage. Yet in response, the Pharisees plot to kill him.

   a. Why do you think they are doing this?

   b. What warning is there for us?

7. How does Jesus' behaviour fulfil the prophecy of Isaiah 42:1-3 (vv. 18-21)?

8. What does this tell us about what the Lord of the Sabbath is like?

To finish

Jesus says the Pharisees are in error because they have not understood what God said in the book of Hosea. There he said, "For I desire steadfast love and not sacrifice, the knowledge of God rather than burnt offerings" (Hos 6:6). How should understanding this affect:

- the way we treat other people?

- the way we treat God?

Give thanks and pray

- Give thanks that Jesus is the Lord of the Sabbath who serves his people gently.
- Pray we would see Jesus rightly and so avoid petty and harsh legalism.

8. JESUS: THE BIG BROTHER YOU WANT

Matthew 12:22-50

Getting started

"It's not what you know but who you know." Do you agree? Why or why not?

Light from the Word

Read Matthew 12:22-50.

1. What do we learn about Jesus from this passage?

2. What do we learn about the Pharisees and teachers of the law from this passage?

3. How does Jesus answer the Pharisees' charge that he is driving out demons by the power of the prince of demons?

4. What encouragement is there here for people who may be anxious about demonic activity?

5. What warning does Jesus give the Pharisees after they have made their charge against him?

6. What evidence is there that the Pharisees had committed the sin against the Holy Spirit?

7. How would you respond to someone who said, "I am worried that I have committed the sin against the Holy Spirit and cannot be forgiven"? (Hint: think about what the Pharisees were doing, and were continuing to do.)

8. In Matthew 7:7 Jesus said, "Ask, and it will be given to you".

   a. Why, then, was it wicked for the Pharisees to ask for a sign (vv. 38-42)?

   b. What will they receive?

9. How would you respond to someone who said, "I just wish God would give me a sign that I should follow Jesus—then I would believe"?

10. The expression 'blood is thicker than water' is sometimes used to mean that family bonds are tighter than other relationships. But how should Jesus' words here (vv. 46-50) affect our thinking about family relationships?

To finish

"Whoever is not with me is against me, and whoever does not gather with me scatters" (Matt 12:30). How should this affect the way we speak?

Give thanks and pray

- Give thanks for the fact that Jesus is stronger than Satan and that he calls all who do the will of his Father his brothers and sisters.
- Pray that our words would not condemn us but would show that we follow the one greater than Solomon and Jonah. Pray for situations where you might be tempted to neither stand with Jesus nor gather with him.

FOR THE LEADER

What are Pathway Bible Guides?

The Pathway Bible Guides aim to provide simple, straightforward Bible study material for:

- Christians who are new to studying the Bible (perhaps because they've been recently converted or because they have joined a Bible study group for the first time)
- Christians who find other studies[1] too much of a stretch.

Accordingly, we've designed the studies to be short, straightforward and easy to use, with a simple vocabulary. At the same time, we've tried to do justice to the passages being studied, and to model good Bible-reading principles. We've tried to be simple without being simplistic; no-nonsense without being no-content.

The questions and answers assume a small group context, but it should be easy to adapt them to suit different situations, such as individual study and one-to-one.

Your role as leader

Because many in your group may not be used to reading and discussing a Bible passage in a group context, a greater level of responsibility will fall to you as the leader of the discussions. There are the usual responsibilities of preparation, prayer and managing group dynamics. In addition, there will be an extra dimension of forming and encouraging good Bible reading habits in people who may not have much of an idea of what those habits look like.

Questions have been kept deliberately brief and simple. For this reason, you may have to fill in some of the gaps that may have been addressed in, say, an Interactive Bible Study. Such 'filling in' may take the form of asking follow-up questions, or using your best judgement to work out when you might need to supply background information. That sort of information, and some suggestions about other questions you could ask, may be found in the following leader's notes. In addition, a *New Bible Dictionary* is always a useful aid to preparation, and simple commentaries such as those in the *Tyndale* or *Bible Speaks Today* series are often helpful. Consult them after you have done your own preparation.

On the question of background information, these studies are written from the assumption that God's word stands alone. God works through his Holy Spirit and the leaders he has gifted—such as you—to make his meaning clear. Assuming this to be true, the best interpreter and provider of background information for Scripture will not be academic historical research, but Scripture itself. Extra historical information may be useful for the purpose of illustration, but it is unnecessary for understanding and applying what God says to us.

The format of the studies

The discussion questions on each passage follow a simple pattern. There is a question at the beginning of each discussion that is intended to get people talking around the issues raised by the passage, and to give you some idea of how people are thinking. If the group turns out to be confident, motivated and comfortable with each other and the task at hand, you may even decide to skip this question. Alternatively, if the group members are shy or quiet, you may decide to think of related types of questions that you could add in to the study, so as to maintain momentum in a non-threatening way.

After the first question, the remaining questions work through the passage sequentially, alternating between observation, interpretation and application in a way that will become obvious when you do your own preparation. The final question of each discussion, just before the opportunity for prayer, could be used in some groups to encourage (say) one person each week to give a short talk (it could be 1 minute or 5 minutes, depending on the topic and the people). The thinking here is that there's no better way to encourage understanding of a passage than to get people to the point where they can explain it to others. Use your judgement in making the best use of this final exercise each week, depending on the people in your group.

In an average group, it should be possible to work through the study in approximately 45 minutes. But it's important that you work out what your group is capable of, given the time available, and make adjustments accordingly. Work out in advance which questions or sub-points can be omitted if time is short. And have a few supplementary questions or discussion starters up your sleeve if your group is dealing with the material quickly and hungering for more. Each group is different. It's your job as leader to use the printed material as 'Bible *Guides*', and not as a set of questions that you must rigidly stick to regardless of your circumstances.

Preparation: 60/40/20

Ideally, group members should spend half an hour reading over the passage and pencilling in some answers *before* they come to the group. Not every group member will do this, of course, but encourage them with the idea that the more they prepare for the study, the more they will get out of the discussion.

In terms of your own preparation as leader, we recommend you put aside approximately *two hours*, either all at once or in two one-hour blocks, and that you divide up the time as follows:

- 60 minutes reading the passage and answering the questions yourself as best you can (without looking at the leader's notes or Bible commentaries)
- 40 minutes consulting the leader's notes (plus other resources, like commentaries). Add to your own answers, and jot down supplementary questions or other information that you want to have available as you lead the discussion. Make sure you write everything you need on the study pages—the last thing you want to do is to keep turning to the 'answers' in the back during the group discussion
- 20 minutes praying about the study and for your group members.

This 60/40/20 pattern will help you to focus on the Bible and what it's saying, rather than simply regurgitating to the group what is in the leader's notes. Remember, these notes are just that—notes to offer some help and guidance. They are not the Bible! As a pattern of preparation, 60/40/20 also helps you to keep praying for yourself and your group, that God would give spiritual growth as his word is sown in your hearts (see Luke 8:4-15; 1 Cor 3:5-7).

If, for some reason, you have less or more time to spend in preparation, simply apply the 60/40/20 proportions accordingly.

1. Such as the Interactive Bible Study (IBS) series also available from Matthias Media.

LEADER'S NOTES

1. JESUS: BEFORE HE WAS FAMOUS

Matthew 7:28-8:27

▶ **Remember: 60/40/20**

Getting started

From unknown beginnings, Jesus quickly became 'newsworthy' and famous. As reports spread, large crowds began to follow him to see what kind of man he was. The chapters we are now turning to record Jesus' initial ministry. When we go back to these early days, we get to see the initial spark that set the flame of his renown spreading. Hence the starter question.

One helpful clue in reading Matthew's Gospel is to realize that there are a number of summary statements sprinkled throughout. For example, Matthew 4:23 gives a summary that anticipates what Jesus will be doing in the early part of his ministry: "teaching ... and proclaiming the gospel of the kingdom" (which we see especially in Matthew 5-7; the Sermon on the Mount) and "healing every disease and every affliction among the people" (which we see in the subsequent chapters, Matthew 8-9).

Then when we reach Matthew 9:35, we find that the summary from 4:23 is repeated almost word for word. This repetition indicates to an attentive reader that we have reached the end of a major section within Matthew's Gospel (that is, 4:23-9:35). As study leader, you may like to draw your group's attention to these summary statements. They help highlight the key features of Jesus' ministry (note also how 4:24-25 draws our attention to the people's response to Jesus).

Studying the passage

Matthew 8-9 (or, strictly, 7:28-9:36) is a section of the Gospel that describes

Jesus' initial ministry 'on the road' in Galilee, preaching and teaching the good news of the kingdom and healing every disease and sickness among the people. The section begins with a statement about the *authority* of Jesus' teaching (7:29) and ends with a statement about his heartfelt *compassion* for the people of Israel (9:36). Throughout this section, both aspects of his ministry are displayed. It is a perfect combination for a man who is both 'good shepherd' and ruler.

We see Jesus' authority in various ways (question 1). A man with leprosy is healed the moment Jesus commands him to be clean (8:3). A centurion's paralysed servant is healed the very hour Jesus says it will be done, even though Jesus is not even in the area (8:5-7, 13)! Jesus heals the sick "with a word" (8:16), and drives out many demons as well. Even the wind and the waves are obedient to his rebuke (8:26-27). No part of creation is beyond Jesus' authority.

The authority of Jesus' *teaching* is also evident in this section. He commands a man to follow him as an even more urgent priority than burying his own father! Yet even as he gives commands to people we realize that there *is* one area of creation that may be resistant to Jesus' authority: the human will. We are not told if the man with leprosy did as Jesus asked, nor whether the next man obeyed Jesus and let others bury his father. Yet the possibility arises that Jesus' authority will be resisted. Jesus even comments, after his encounter with the centurion, that the sons of the kingdom "will be thrown into the outer darkness" (8:12)!

Jesus also shows remarkable compassion (question 2). While the leper may have been uncertain about Jesus' willingness to cleanse him, Jesus' touch and declaration make his willingness plain. His compassion for the centurion is striking: here is a Gentile commander of a foreign army, currently ruling over and oppressing Israel. Yet Jesus responds to even his plea. His compassion reaches not only those close to him (8:14-15) but also the multitudes. The passage gives the impression that though it was late at night, he turned no-one away (8:16).

This healing activity of Jesus in Galilee is explained in verse 17 (question 2b). This verse contains what is known as a 'fulfilment formula' ("This was to fulfil what was spoken by the prophet ...") and it is common in Matthew's Gospel.[1]

In a 'fulfilment formula', an event in Jesus' life is not just reported as a bald fact. Rather, the event is linked to an important Old Testament prophecy or promise. Very often we find that the verses quoted are just one small line from a well-known and significant part of the Old Testament. Matthew 8:17 is no exception, for here Matthew quotes a snippet from the prophet Isaiah (find the original passage—Isaiah 52:13-53:12—and ask someone to read it out to the group).

When we dig into this quote from Isaiah, we discover that it is an extremely important prophecy about God's anointed servant. Indeed, it is hardly an exaggeration to say that Matthew has quoted one of the most important prophecies in the entire Old Testament. The servant in the Isaiah 52-53 prophecy comes to serve his people and to suffer for their sake. He not only suffers, but he also takes their sin, pain and uncleanness upon himself.

In other words, these verses in Isaiah are no less than a promise about what is going to happen when Jesus dies on the cross. By using the Old Testament in this way, Matthew is actually preaching the cross of Christ!

Questions 3-4 pick up on the way various people respond to events. In particular, and twice in this passage, we read about *Jesus'* response to people's responses. Jesus marvels at the centurion because he, more than anyone, has grasped Jesus' authority. This is indeed a marvel, as the centurion is not an Israelite and knows nothing of Israel's God. As a powerful army commander, he could even have tried lording it over Jesus. But he does nothing of the sort. Instead, he humbly recognizes his standing before Jesus (8:8). Jesus also expresses surprise (at the very least) at his own disciples. In contrast to the centurion's faith, these disciples—who had seen more evidence of Jesus' authority—only had "little faith" (8:26). The study ends, then, with questions focusing on how we ought to respond to Jesus' authority and compassion (questions 5-6).

Jesus' statement that "the Son of Man has nowhere to lay his head" is surprising. It is clear that Jesus has authority over all of creation—and yet even foxes have a more permanent home than he does! If the quotation from Isaiah 53 is properly understood, it is not as surprising, however. As Jesus himself will explain, the Son of Man has come not to be served, but to serve and give his life as a ransom. Since no servant is above their master, then Jesus' disciples ought not have any expectations of permanent dwellings in this world. Jesus' words here challenge our views about the priority of property and housing. Question 4b provides an opportunity for groups to feel the weight of Jesus' challenge.

Jesus' statement, "Follow me, and leave the dead to bury their own dead" is equally challenging and arresting. In the Old Testament, the chief priest was not to leave the sanctuary to bury his parents (see Lev 21:10-15). Jesus is implying that being with him is as important as meeting with God himself in the sanctuary; nothing is to take priority over it. This again challenges our tendency to give our family our first allegiance. Question 5b is aimed at provoking your group members to consider how they might rightly give their first allegiance to Jesus before family.

There are other indications in this passage about what it means to follow Jesus, most notably in Jesus' dealings with the centurion. Following Jesus clearly means having faith in him and acknowledging his authority. The incident during the storm suggests this, and also suggests that his disciples ought not to fear those things over which Jesus has authority.

To finish

After Jesus calms the storm, his disciples ask one another, "What sort of man is this ...?" The disciples presumably included at least the four fishermen mentioned in Matthew 4:18-22. The question was therefore one asked between workmates, which is why part of the final question asks people to consider how their own workmates would answer this question. The second question aims to get people to summarize what they think this passage teaches about "what sort of man" this is. It is clear that Jesus is God's promised king, indeed God himself, whose great authority is matched only by his compassion. The final question is aimed at challenging your group members to match their lives to their assessment of Jesus.

1. See 1:22, 2:17, 2:23 and 4:13-16 for other examples from earlier in Matthew.

LEADER'S NOTES

2. JESUS: DOCTOR TO SINNERS

Matthew 8:28-9:36

▶ **Remember: 60/40/20**

Getting started

In this passage, Jesus comes to people who are morally and spiritually sick. He casts himself as a 'doctor to the spiritually sick' who provides a cure for their ills. The opening question is to get people thinking about these themes and people's attitudes to them in our society.

Studying the passage

We have already said in study 1 that Matthew 8-9 forms a unit within the Gospel (see the leader's notes for that study). For that reason we highlight the links between this passage and the previous one (7:28-8:27) by again looking for evidence of Jesus' authority and his compassion. In these verses, there is a great deal of evidence for both.

Question 1 asks readers for examples of Jesus' authority and compassion. As you work through, note also the beginnings of opposition (a new element here in Matthew's Gospel, although it was anticipated by Jesus' childhood experience as a refugee). You may wish to fill in question 1 as you read through each of the different sections of this passage.

Jesus displays his authority by casting out fierce demons with a single word. Their subservience to him speaks of this authority. His authority to heal and to forgive sins is revealed in the healing of the paralytic. Matthew's simple obedience to Jesus' command shows Jesus' authority. Jesus' responses to the Pharisees and John the Baptist's disciples authoritatively address the concerns they raise. He heals several people towards the end of the chapter with a simple word—curing chronic illnesses, raising the dead, curing the blind and driving out demons. The crowd sums up how his authority compares to others: "Never was anything like this seen in Israel" (9:33).

Equally, Jesus' compassion is on display—often alongside his authority. The demon-possessed men in the Gadarenes could easily have been avoided. Jesus cares for the tax collectors and sinners, in the face of mockery. He defends his disciples. He speaks tenderly to the woman with the flow of blood, whom he heals, and does what the ruler pleads. And he has mercy on the blind men, as they request.

But we see also the emergence of opposition. Jesus is asked to leave the region of the Gadarenes. The scribes grumble that Jesus is blaspheming when he forgives sins. The Pharisees quiz the disciples about Jesus' behaviour, and furthermore conclude that "He casts out demons by the prince of demons" (9:34).

Question 2 focuses on response. The demons, for example, acknowledge Jesus' power and plead with him. The Gadarenes ask him to leave. The paralytic and his friends have faith, as does the ruler, the woman with the discharge and the two blind men. The scribes consider him to be blaspheming. John's disciples misunderstand him. The Pharisees regard him as a friend of sinners and in league with the devil. The crowd marvel at him and glorify God because of his deeds. Matthew follows him. Jesus' judgement upon various responses highlights which ones we are to imitate, and it would be good to draw your group's attention to this.

Question 3 draws attention to the unusual response of the people of the Gadarenes. It is unusual because while they recognize Jesus' power, they do not trust his goodness. Neither, however, does their opposition to him seem to be as overt as that of the Pharisees. Yet the effect is the same: they reject him and wish to carry on life without him. It seems that they are too afraid that Jesus will upset the status quo—being more alarmed by the death of the pigs (perhaps for financial or superstitious reasons) than joyful at the wonder of two demon-possessed men being cured. While there are many incidents in this passage, the response of the Gadarenes gets particular attention in our study because even today, it is a common yet more subtle way of opposing and dismissing Jesus.

Matthew 9:36 summarizes the condition of the people of Israel as being "like sheep without a shepherd". Jesus' attitude towards them is characterized as having "compassion for them". This summary echoes Ezekiel 36, suggesting that Matthew wants us to see Jesus' entire ministry in Galilee as fulfilling this prophecy. The idea of returning to the Old Testament in questions 4 and 5 is to show how Jesus fulfils God's Old Testament promises.

In Ezekiel 36:1-6, God compares Israel's leaders to shepherds, and condemns the leaders for feeding themselves and failing to feed and care for their sheep. The sheep are vulnerable—"harassed and helpless", as Jesus will call them. So in Ezekiel 36:11-16, God promises that *he himself* will come to care for their sheep. He will seek the lost, bind up the injured and strengthen the weak. Then Jesus comes, doing what God has promised he would do. He is 'doctor to the sinners'—calling sinners like Matthew, binding up injured people like the woman with the flow of blood, and strengthening the weak like the paralysed man.

The final 'Light from the Word' question draws out a truth that we often fail to acknowledge—that our assessment of Jesus reflects on the character of the one making the assessment, even more than it reflects on Jesus. The paralytic and his friends see their great need of Jesus. Matthew similarly has no problem recognizing he is sick and that he needs to be healed of his sins. The woman with the flow of blood and the ruler, even though they are at opposite ends of the social spectrum, both know themselves to be desperate. The blind men can nonetheless see that they don't deserve to be healed by Jesus.

However, it is not only the positive responses that reflect on the ones responding. The response of the Gadarenes shows that they did not believe they needed Jesus. The Pharisees' indignation in 8:11 shows that they did not see themselves as sick sinners needing a doctor. The disciples of John did not think they had cause to rejoice in Jesus' coming. The aim of questions 5b and c is to emphasize that neither our response to Jesus nor those of people we know are objective but are shaped by our assessment of ourselves. In part, this is an encouragement to rightly see ourselves as 'sinners needing a doctor'.

To finish

The first finishing question presents something of a riddle. While it may surprise us, Jesus had come to call the Pharisees as well—for they too were sinners. However, Jesus' *method* of calling is very revealing. In saying that he has not come to call the righteous but sinners, he sifts out those who do not think they need mercy. Jesus calls the Pharisees—but they will not hear his call if they do not see themselves as sinners. This is a warning to us. Unless we see ourselves as sinners needing mercy, we will not rightly appreciate our need for Jesus. Nor will we heed his call, nor rejoice at his coming.

LEADER'S NOTES

3. JESUS: LORD OF THE HARVEST

Matthew 9:35-10:23

▶ **Remember: 60/40/20**

Getting started

In this passage, Jesus sends his disciples on a mission to replicate his ministry throughout Israel. He prepares them for this and further ministry by giving them right expectations about what it will be like. The passage therefore teaches us much about having the right expectations of what being a disciple of Jesus involves. The 'Getting started' question gets people thinking about the importance of having right expectations.

Studying the passage

Matthew 4:23-9:36 is one section in Matthew where the authority of Jesus' words is evident. The authority of his words continues to be evident whenever he speaks, however, and question 1 provides continuity with the previous two studies by again drawing attention to this.

Jesus' authority is evident in his understanding of the situation in Israel and in his knowledge of what is required. It is further evident in the task that he gives to the disciples, in which he effectively authorizes *them* to do the work he has been doing in Israel. He has complete awareness of the nature of the opposition his disciples will face for the sake of his name, and this lends authority to what he says; likewise his recommendations for how they are to endure this opposition.

Jesus gives the disciples a specific task. They are not to go among the Gentiles or to any Samaritan towns; they are only to go "to the lost sheep of the house of Israel" (10:6). Their task appears to replicate the ministry that we have seen Jesus doing in chapters 8-9. They are to proclaim the same message which Jesus (4:17), and before him, John the Baptist (3:2), have been proclaiming: "The kingdom of heaven is at hand" (see 10:7). Jesus' authorization of his disciples in Matthew 10:1 to "heal every disease and every affliction" matches the language of the summary in 9:35, and his command in 10:8 that they "Heal the sick, raise the dead, cleanse lepers, cast out demons" summarizes precisely what he has been doing.

This is an urgent task. Jesus tells them that they will not have gone through all the towns of Israel before the Son of Man comes. This expression picks up the prophecy in Daniel 7:13-14 of "one like a son of man" who goes to the "Ancient of Days" and is given "dominion and glory and a kingdom" so that all the people on earth should serve him. In his closing words in Matthew's Gospel, Jesus begins, "All authority in heaven and on earth has been given to me. Go therefore and make disciples of all nations ..." (Matt 28:18-19). It is clear from these closing words that in one sense at least the Son of Man has 'come' (or rather 'gone to the Ancient of Days') by the end of the Gospel. The urgency of the task is also suggested by Jesus' commands that they 'travel light' (10:9-10), and by the instruction to exit swiftly from places that do not receive them (10:14, 23).

The reason Jesus appoints the disciples to this task flows out of his compassion. In his compassion, he has seen that the crowds are harassed and helpless, having no shepherd to care for them. He appoints his disciples as 'labourers' for the harvest field and 'shepherds' for the lost sheep of Israel. It is interesting to note that the very ones he encourages to pray for more labourers in the harvest field are the same ones who are sent into it.

While Jesus' comment in 9:37 that "The harvest is plentiful, but the labourers are few" was specifically about the situation in Israel, it nevertheless contains a principle: the way to maximize the harvest is to have sufficient workers. The way to get more workers is to ask the Lord of the harvest for them. Questions 4-5 are designed to help people see this principle and consider what action it requires of them.

Jesus says several things to the disciples about how they are to go about their task (question 6). They are to give as freely as they themselves have received. Yet they will be provided for, so they are to travel light. They are to discriminate between houses and towns they enter, remaining in those that welcome them and rejecting those that reject them. They are also to be wary. Given that they will be persecuted, Jesus does not encourage them to stand and fight in the face of persecution, but to flee to the next town because the time is short.

Acknowledging that some places will not receive or listen to his disciples' words leads Jesus to then warn his disciples about the realities of the situation they are going into (question 7). It is not a friendly environment; it will be hostile. Jesus sends them as sheep among wolves. Jesus warns that people will hand them over to authorities, and even those closest to them will not be above handing them over to death. In saying "you will be hated by all for my name's sake", Jesus appears to mean that they will be hated by all *types* of people, even family. Jesus' warning that the disciples will be handed over to kings and bear witness to Gentiles raises the question about whether he is still speaking of the immediate task. It seems Jesus is saying that the mission to Israel will give the disciples a foretaste of their later ministry.

This passage contains many useful and important principles for Christian ministry. Most ministers like it to be known that the labourer deserves his food. Yet at the same time, most ministers would protest if told they were not allowed more than one of each item of clothing! Jesus' words raise a dilemma. While some things are to be taken as principles for Christian ministry (e.g. the labourer deserves his food), other things are not (e.g. it is *not* every Christian worker's task to 'raise the dead'—10:8!). The dilemma is resolved by recalling that, first and foremost, Jesus is giving the disciples a specific task. Question 8 aims, therefore, to draw out the things that are specific to the disciples' task, and to see which things are common to all Christian ministry.

There are many things in Jesus' commissioning of his disciples that apply only to them. By the end of Matthew's Gospel Jesus will commission them to go to all nations, and not only to the lost sheep of Israel. It is clear from elsewhere in the Gospels (Luke 22:35-36) that the commands about travelling light were only related to the urgency of the task. It is also clear that Jesus' personal authorization of the disciples to do the same miracles he has been doing has not been given to every believer. Similarly, the commanded responses to various towns and houses appear related to the context of the times Jesus' disciples were in, and the urgency of their task.

This does not mean, however, that Jesus has nothing to say here about other Christian ministry. For example, since we also receive the blessings of the kingdom freely, we also should freely share the news of the kingdom. Similarly, those who labour at sharing the gospel are worthy of support, while those who do not receive gospel labourers are in danger of judgement. All types of people hate followers of Jesus because of him, and so all Christians are also like sheep among wolves and need to be aware that they may well be betrayed and persecuted by those who they might expect to be on their side. This is what Jesus means when he commands his disciples to be "wise as serpents". They are not to naively think that everyone will be supportive of them and on their side. They are to be realistic: even their own family members may hand them over to be persecuted.

Given the severity of the persecution anticipated by Jesus in this section, it is right to ask, "Is it worth it?" Question 10 tries to get people to feel the weight of this question, given the terrifying nature of the warnings Jesus gives. Two things indicate that following Jesus will be well worth it. In verse 15, Jesus makes it clear that a more terrible judgement awaits those who reject him. But those who persevere in following Jesus have nothing to fear regarding this judgement. In verse 22, Jesus makes it clear that all who endure following him to the end will be saved from it.

To finish

While Jesus' warnings in this passage may sound dire and extreme, they speak of reality. Thus, they are very kind. To be given false expectations is to be set up for crushing disappointment and discouragement. To be given *right* expectations is to be rightly equipped for the task. Jesus gives his disciples no illusions about how difficult it will be following him. Yet he also makes it clear that they will be looked after by one another. And, more importantly, on the day of judgement it will all be well and truly worth it.

LEADER'S NOTES

4. JESUS: THE ONE TO FEAR

Matthew 10:24-42

▶ Remember: 60/40/20

Getting started

In this passage, Jesus gives reasons why his disciples need not fear those who persecute them (see verses 26, 28 and 31). Hence the 'Getting started' question introduces the theme of fear, and encourages your group members to think about how to overcome it. The idea is to provide a useful point of contrast and comparison for later in the study.

Studying the passage

Questions 1-2 give an overview. Here are some useful observations.

Jesus continues to equip his disciples for persecution. Part of the way he does that is by continuing to give them realistic expectations about what it will be like to be his disciple. They will be treated no differently to him—if he has been called Beelzebul, so will they. His coming will also bring the sword of division to the closest of relationships.

However, Jesus spells out not only the difficulties of being his disciple, but also the benefits. Jesus will treat people before his Father in heaven as they have treated him before other people. Those who lose their life for Jesus will save it, while those who do not will lose it. Those who receive even the least of Jesus' disciples in the smallest possible way will not go unrewarded.

It would be easy to get distracted by a discussion about 'rewards': whether it is possible for Christians to merit rewards, and how this may then square with a doctrine of justification by grace alone and through faith alone. Since Jesus' words in verses 40-42 are clearly aimed at encouraging *practical* hospitality to Jesus' messengers and his disciples, it would be best not to get too sidetracked by these discussions here. Given that the one who receives the least of Jesus' disciples ultimately receives the one who sent Jesus, the reward Jesus is speaking of may well be that both the Son and the Father welcome the disciple into the kingdom of heaven (as verse 32 implies; 25:31-40 also suggests this). This is not to say that salvation is by works, but rather the salvation disciples receive will be consistent with their discipleship.

Throughout, Jesus simply assumes that he is great and powerful. He sees himself as the head of the house (presumably of Israel), the true master and teacher. He regards God the Father as *his* father. He claims to decide who his Father accepts or rejects. He speaks of himself as being worthy of people's ultimate loyalty, even over their own families and lives. Receiving him is the same as receiving God himself!

Question 3 explores which parts of what Jesus says are specific to the disciples, and which parts relate to Christians today. While everything Jesus says is directed first and foremost to the disciples, what he says broadens in its application as Matthew's Gospel unfolds. So while we saw in 10:5-15 many things that were particular to the context of the twelve apostles at the time, the verses in this passage speak more generally to the situation of all disciples of Jesus.

Questions 4-9 explore why the disciples (or anyone who has a body!) are not to fear those who persecute them. There are at least three reasons. The first is that hidden things will be revealed. Those who secretly plot evil will be exposed; their thoughts and deeds will be broadcast for all to hear. Second (v. 28), it is because one who is more fearsome ought to be feared more. One fear is to be overcome by a greater fear—here the one who can destroy not only the body but both body and soul in hell. In the parables of Matthew 13 Jesus will make it clear that it is the Son of Man (that is, himself) who is able to do this (see Matt 13:41-42). The third reason Jesus gives not to fear is that in his sovereignty, nothing escapes God's care or notice—and the Father cares deeply for his disciples. Further encouragements not to fear are given in the passage: Jesus will acknowledge before his Father those who acknowledge him before people, and those who lose their lives for Jesus' sake will in fact save them. Question 10 applies these priorities to the family.

Question 11 aims to tease out the implications of Jesus' challenging words in verses 37-39. Jesus says "whoever loses his life *for my sake …*"; he is not encouraging random sacrifice.

Jesus finishes by promising that any who show the least concern to someone—because they are Jesus' disciple—will not go unrewarded. The explanation is in verse 42: "because he is a disciple". Jesus is not simply saying that anyone who gives any other human a drink will be rewarded. It is a wonderful encouragement, because it indicates that even the smallest kindness to the least of Jesus' disciples does not go unnoticed by God.

To finish

The final question asks people to apply Jesus' teaching to how we ourselves can support 'disciples'—friends in church; people being persecuted for their faith here or elsewhere; gospel teachers who are being supported locally or overseas.

LEADER'S NOTES

5. JESUS: DON'T LOOK FOR ANOTHER

Matthew 11:1-19

▶ Remember: 60/40/20

Getting started

This passage begins in a curious fashion. John the Baptist sends a question to Jesus from prison, via his disciples, asking Jesus whether he is the one to come or whether they should look for another. Either John the Baptist or his disciples, or both, have doubts about Jesus. In this passage, then, we get to hear Jesus dealing with people's doubts. His approach can both help dispel our own doubts and help us deal with other people's doubts about him. The 'Getting started' question introduces these ideas.

Studying the passage

This passage deals with Jesus and his relationship to John the Baptist. We can easily underrate the importance of this relationship. Yet Jesus makes plain that this relationship helps us correctly know his identity.

Matthew 3:11-12 provides important background information that helps us understand the disciples' question and Jesus' response; hence, question 1. The verses show how John understood that the one coming after him would be far greater than he was. He expected the one to come to baptize people with the Holy Spirit (a sign of salvation) and with fire (a sign of judgement). It seems he expected the one to come to gather his people and bring judgement upon those who were unrepentant.

John's disciples ask Jesus whether he is the one to come or whether they should look for another. It is not clear whether it was John or his disciples who were wondering this, but in the end it is immaterial. The fact that John was still in prison may have prompted the question. Perhaps John or his disciples expected him to 'clear away the chaff' immediately. John or his disciples may not have understood why the wicked continued to flourish and the righteous continued to suffer, if Jesus was the one to come. (Jesus will go on to explain in the parable of the weeds in Matthew 13:24-30 that while the kingdom has begun, the harvest at the end of the age, where evil is dealt with, is still to come.)

Jesus' answer is revealing. He tells John's disciples to report back to John tangible things: things they can see and hear. They are eyewitnesses, who see that those who are not offended by Jesus are blessed—they are healed, cleansed, raised from the dead and have good news preached to them. This shows how Jesus approaches people's doubts: he deals with them by pointing to eyewitness evidence.

Yet Jesus' answer reveals far more, for his response is rich with Old Testament allusions. The language he uses picks up the language of Isaiah 35:3-6 and Isaiah 61:1, which are passages that speak about the coming of the Messiah and the great messianic age. Be sure to look these passages up so that group members can see the connections. Jesus is effectively saying that "the evidence testifies that the kingdom of the Messiah has arrived". It may be difficult to get the group to fully appreciate the significance of the way Jesus is pointing to the fulfilment of the Old Testament. However, the idea is to help people see that Jesus both points to tangible evidence, and argues from the promises of the Old Testament, to prove who he is.

As John the Baptist's disciples leave, Jesus continues speaking to the crowds about him. Jesus identifies the man who preached in the wilderness, and lived an austere life, as a true prophet who was a man of substance (vv. 7-9). He is unlike "those who wear soft clothing ... in kings' houses" (most likely a veiled criticism of Herod and those who had imprisoned John). Indeed, Jesus calls John the greatest among those born of women.

Jesus adds that John is far more than a prophet. John, teaches Jesus, is the one identified by Old Testament prophecy (specifically, Malachi) as the 'messenger' and 'Elijah';[1] the one who prepares the way for Jesus. John is the 'last of the prophets', the 'Elijah' who brings the final prophecy to Israel.

This is the reason for questions 4-5. In Malachi 3:1, God himself promised that he would come to the temple (both to save and to judge, according to Malachi 3:2-4). Before all this happens, God promises that he will send a messenger. This messenger, 'Elijah', will come before the great and dreadful day of the Lord. Elijah will "turn the hearts of fathers to their children and the hearts of children to their fathers", meaning that he will call them to repentance—as John does. When they do not repent, John curses them (see Matt 3:1-10). The startling thing about Jesus identifying John the Baptist as the 'messenger' and 'Elijah', then, is what it says about who Jesus is: he is the God of Israel come to visit his people (note that he will go on to speak of judgement and salvation in this chapter from 11:20-30).

Jesus finishes speaking to the crowd about John with his familiar call: "He who has ears to hear, let him hear" (v. 15). This curious expression is an emphatic command to listen carefully. The parable of the sower will give further insight into what this command means, but at this point it is clear that Jesus is inviting those who are willing to listen to hear and perceive what he is saying (namely, that he is the Lord who visits after 'Elijah').

Jesus' comment in verse 12 is difficult and may raise questions. It would be wise not to let these questions sidetrack the group from understanding the heart of what Jesus is saying about John the Baptist. Of the many meanings possible for this verse, the preferred one is that from the time of John the Baptist until this point in Jesus' ministry, the kingdom of God has been forcefully advancing. This activity is contrasted in the second half of the verse by the activity of "the violent" who are trying to take or destroy it by force—for example, by putting John in prison. On this understanding, Jesus is explaining why the kingdom of heaven has been advancing yet at the same time John the Baptist is put in prison.

Jesus does not hold out much hope that his generation will have ears to hear (question 7). He points out that while he and John the Baptist had the same message, they had very different approaches. Yet Jesus' generation had complaints about both approaches. The song the children sing in verse 17 seems to emphasize that no matter what tune is played, people were not happy. Nor are those happy who do not want to repent at the coming of the kingdom; they will reject the messenger no matter how they bring the message. Jesus' comment that "wisdom is justified by her deeds" suggests that both John's and Jesus' approaches were appropriate in their different circumstances.

To finish

This is not one of the most familiar passages in Matthew's Gospel. Yet, like the rest of the Gospel, it offers a persuasive argument that Jesus is the promised

Messiah—indeed, that he is God himself. It does this in particular by pointing to the verifiable nature of Jesus' miracles and how they fulfilled Old Testament expectation. This final exercise is intended to get people to try to see how this passage can be used to address people's doubts about Jesus.

1. Elijah is one of the greatest of God's Old Testament prophets. When Elijah is present, it is clear that God is at work through his message. John the Baptist even dresses like Elijah (Matt 3:4; compare 2 Kgs 1:8)!

LEADER'S NOTES

6. JESUS: THE WAY TO FIND REST

Matthew 11:20-30

▶ Remember: 60/40/20

Getting started

In this passage, Jesus invites people to come to him to find rest for their souls. And yet the passage begins by Jesus pronouncing a terrible judgement upon his hometown and other cities near where he lived. The 'Getting started' question aims to help people start thinking about this contrast.

Studying the passage

Jesus mentions the response to his ministry, and to that of John the Baptist. He then gives two starkly contrasting speeches. In the first, he speaks the strongest possible word of judgement against certain cities. In the second, he offers some of the most gentle and soothing statements contained in the Gospel. The difference between the two speeches could not be more extreme.

Matthew 4:23-9:35 records Jesus' ministry around his home region of Galilee. In Matthew 10, Jesus then commissions his disciples to go to the lost sheep of Israel. Matthew 11:1 records that after instructing the disciples, Jesus then went and preached in their cities. It is clear that by now, the cities of Galilee have had a good opportunity to hear and receive Jesus' ministry—if they have ears to hear.

However, judging by Jesus' words in Matthew 11:20-24, the cities in Galilee have *not* had ears to hear. We are told in Matthew 4:13 that Jesus had moved to Capernaum to live. The cities of Bethsaida and Chorazin were nearby cities around the sea of Galilee. Verse 20 indicates that these were the cities in which most of his mighty works had been done. And yet it is clear that in spite of this, they did not repent. Jesus therefore declares that they will receive a more severe judgement than even the most notorious cities of the Old Testament—Tyre and Sidon (which were consumed by fire) and Sodom (which was destroyed by sulphur).

Jesus' denunciation of these cities is extraordinary. The cities of Tyre and Sidon were places full of violence and bloodshed. Sodom was a city where pack rapes went unpunished. There is little evidence that such horrific activities had been taking place in Chorazin, Bethsaida or Capernaum. What had they done that was so wrong?

The answer comes in Jesus' twice repeated expression: "if the mighty works done in you ..." (11:21, 23). These cities have witnessed the most extraordinary revelation of God. Indeed, the revelation is so spectacular that Jesus says it would have caused the notorious cities of Tyre, Sidon and Sodom to repent. And yet these towns of Jesus' neighbourhood stubbornly refused to repent at his preaching. Jesus' strong denunciation in these verses underscores the biblical principle—to whom much is given, much is expected (e.g. Luke 12:48; cf. 1 Pet 4:17).

Jesus' fierce condemnation in these verses carries a strong warning to us and shakes us out of our complacency. From those who know the ministry of Jesus well—perhaps through family, school, church or through studying to prepare a Bible study—more will be expected. Failure to repent at the ministry of Jesus will result in condemnation, and that condemnation will be most severe for those who know the most about Jesus' ministry. Question 3 provides an opportunity to warn those whose familiarity with the gospel may have bred some contempt.

Having spoken words of the utmost condemnation, Jesus then speaks some of the most wonderful words of consolation. He begins in verses 25-26 with a prayer. The prayer acknowledges that according to the kind will of the Father, knowledge of the Father and the Son is hidden from the wise and learned and revealed to little children. This is not discrimination against the educated. Rather it is discrimination against those who are arrogant; it is the humble who are given insight. Jesus makes it clear that people cannot know the Father unless they first know Jesus and Jesus then chooses to reveal the Father to them.

This passage has much to say then about people's knowledge of God. Question 5 tries to draw these things out. On the one hand, people are unable of themselves to know what God the Father is like; it can only come by revelation. On the other hand, it is not right to say that "we can't know what God is like"—for the Son knows what the Father is like. And if the Son chooses to reveal the Father to people, then they too know what God is like.

Verses 28-30 reveal further things about Jesus. He is a kind and gentle master, humble in heart. He is able to provide rest for people's souls, and his way is not burdensome. Questions 6-9 are intended to mine some of the precious jewels that are to be found in these few verses. Jesus' commands are simple: "Come to me" and "Take my yoke upon you, and learn from me". The image of the yoke is that of a wooden guide which would go around the necks of oxen as they ploughed. Yet Jesus makes it clear that his yoke is more a help than a burden.

Significantly, he gives the command to "all who labour and are heavy laden". It is a very broad invitation. It is given to all. Those invited to come do not need to be perfect, wise or religious. It is an invitation to those who are weary and burdened. We may assume that many of the people who have already come to Jesus in Matthew's Gospel fit this description: the paralytic whose sins were forgiven, the demon-possessed, the snubbed tax collectors, the sinners, the grieving ruler and the agonized centurion. Indeed, even the Pharisees, if they had eyes to see it, were burdened and wearied by their own legalism, and they put a heavy yoke on others. Those burdened by the words of judgement Jesus had just spoken would also be included. It would be good to spend time pushing people on question 7 to realize how broad Jesus' invitation is.

The assurances Jesus gives to those who obey his command to 'come' are most comforting. He promises rest for weary souls. Rest is something that has been elusive for humans ever since the fall, and in the context here (after Jesus has just spoken of judgement), rest is a picture of salvation. Although Jesus does not say it, his earlier words indicate that those who do not come to him will face judgement. Question 9 is designed to ensure that Jesus' wonderful words in verse 25-30 are considered in the context of his words in verses 21-24.

Question 10 returns to the 'Getting started' question and gets your group members to consider how Jesus' way to rest is unusual. It is particularly unusual in that he promises to simply provide it himself, and nothing is required except approaching him.

To finish

Jesus' statements that his yoke is easy and his burden is light are clearly intended as an incentive. His self-recommendation that he is gentle and lowly in heart does the same. Yet they also indicate that those who "labour and are heavy laden" are often suspicious of Jesus—they think that his way is in fact more burdensome, and that he is not out to help us but to subject us to harsh slavery. Nothing could be further from the truth, and the finishing question is meant to help people realize this.

LEADER'S NOTES

7. JESUS: THE LORD OF REST

Matthew 11:28-12:21

▶ **Remember: 60/40/20**

Getting started

The 'Getting started' question may promote a discussion between those who think more easily of the 'big picture' and those who find it easier to focus on details. A discussion of this sort may well be helpful, perhaps leading people to realize that attention needs to be paid to both and that one must not be forgotten when focusing on the other. This topic is related to the main theme of the passage. The Pharisees make terrible mistakes in applying the details of the law, about which they are so meticulous, because they miss the greater issue: that the Lord of the Sabbath is among them.

Studying the passage

Jesus' words in Matthew 11:28-30 (where he shows that his yoke is easy and his burden is light) lead into his next encounter with the Pharisees. Jesus allows his hungry disciples to pluck grain on the Sabbath. He also treats the man with the withered hand with respect and compassion.

Jesus' yoke is in stark contrast to that of the Pharisees, whose yoke is harsh and whose burden is heavy. Question 1c tries to get readers to see this contrast. The Pharisees condemn the innocent disciples. Whether the law actually forbade the disciples to pluck heads of grain on the Sabbath is itself debatable. In Exodus 23:10-11, Moses had said that Israelites were to leave their fields unused on the Sabbath so that foreigners and the poor could walk through them and collect food. Arguably, the disciples could have been counted among the poor who were permitted to collect grain on the Sabbath. Yet the Pharisees' lack of compassion leads them to condemn the innocent. Despite their fastidiousness about laws relating to work on the Sabbath, they have no problem plotting murder on the Sabbath! They hypocritically ask insincere questions—not wishing to know the answer, but rather to provide an opportunity to accuse Jesus. This callous lack of compassion blinds them from seeing Jesus for who he really is, and leads them to plot his destruction.

In his response to the Pharisees' charge, Jesus points out both the Pharisees' lack of compassion and their blindness to his true identity. In doing so, Jesus reveals more about himself (cf. Matt 11:25-27). He also explains why his disciples are innocent.

Firstly, he implies that he is at least equal to if not greater than David (12:3-4). To show this, Jesus refers to an incident recorded in 1 Samuel 21:1-6, where David and his companions went into the temple and ate the bread which was consecrated only for the priests to eat. The bread was still in the temple, which suggests that it was the Sabbath when David did this. The significance of the story lies not simply in that there were some people in the Old Testament who were permitted to do what was "not lawful to do on the Sabbath" because they were hungry. The real significance is that what they did was acceptable because David, the Messiah,[1] was with them. The implication is that 'a Messiah greater than David' is present in Jesus, and so his disciples were not doing anything unlawful.

Secondly, Jesus states more directly that he is greater than the temple (12:6). In Numbers 28:9-11, the priests were commanded to perform duties that amounted to working on the Sabbath. Yet Jesus explains that this was permissible according to the Law, because they were serving in the temple. The principle assumed is that service in the temple overrides the commands about rest on the Sabbath. Jesus says that he is greater than the temple—and therefore his disciples are permitted to do 'work' on the Sabbath in his presence. Because he is greater than the Sabbath, Jesus is the Lord of the Sabbath: he can determine what is and is not lawful on it.

In both cases, understanding who Jesus is in large part explains Jesus' defence of his disciples' innocence. This is why question 2 asks what else we learn about Jesus in the passage. The information gained in answering this will equip your group members to understand why Jesus calls his disciples innocent (question 3). However, the passage reveals even more about Jesus, and question 2 aims to get people to look for these things also. For example, Jesus' courage is shown in the face of the Pharisees' accusing question. His compassion is shown to the man with the withered hand. His shrewdness is shown in his withdrawal from the synagogue, and his popularity is demonstrated by the multitudes that followed him. Finally, as Matthew points out with another 'fulfilment formula', Jesus' actions in this section demonstrate that he is the 'suffering servant' promised in the book of Isaiah.

Jesus gives another reason why the Pharisees have condemned the innocent in 12:7. He says that they have not known the meaning of Hosea 6:6, which says: "I desire steadfast love and not sacrifice". By this he most likely means not that they did not know this *verse*, but rather that they had failed to grasp its sense and respond rightly to it. In Hosea, the priests were observing the Old Testament sacrificial laws while simultaneously plotting murder. Through Hosea, God says that he would prefer they showed steadfast love to people, rather than make sacrifices as they schemed to kill. The Pharisees have ignored God's desires.

The Pharisees, then, have condemned those God regards as innocent. The reason is that they lacked compassion for the innocent, and this harshness has blinded them from seeing Jesus for who he really is—the Lord of the Sabbath. Their failure to have compassion and to recognize Jesus led them to continue in their harsh legalism. It is a legalism that is all too easy for those who profess to uphold the Bible! Questions 4-5 try to get people thinking about how and why we might fall into the same trap as the Pharisees.

As one sin often leads to another greater sin, so with the Pharisees in this passage. Their condemnation of the innocent disciples leads to their plot to destroy Jesus. Their behaviour is shocking. Jesus performs a miracle. Yet on the very same Sabbath that they appear so eager to observe, they plot to murder the Lord of the Sabbath! Again, their negative example provides a warning (question 6b). Exactly why the Pharisees plot to kill Jesus is not stated. However one sin has led to another; and lack of compassion has led to a murder plot. Jealousy and pride no doubt contributed to their behaviour too (though this text does not say that).

The passage finishes with Jesus withdrawing from the synagogue, and healing the multitudes that follow him. Matthew indicates that this fulfils the prophesy of Isaiah 42. The passage quoted from Isaiah is the first of what have become known as the 'Servant Songs' (the others are Isaiah 49:1-7 and Isaiah 52:13-53:12; Isaiah 61 is sometimes regarded as a fourth servant song). These 'songs' speak of a 'servant' who will act on behalf of Israel to restore her fortunes.

It is somewhat ambiguous initially in Isaiah whether this servant is an individual or a remnant within Israel or even Israel itself. Yet as the songs progress it becomes clearer and clearer that the servant is in fact the Messiah, God's chosen king over Israel. The servant songs then indicate the type of Messiah who will come and redeem Israel. He is a gentle servant (as the quote in Matthew emphasizes). This quote also shows that the Lord of the Sabbath will ultimately bring in a righteous kingdom that will even bring hope to the Gentiles. This quote from Isaiah at this point in Matthew's Gospel, then, indicates both the manner and scope of the Messiah Jesus' reign.

To finish

This passage presents Jesus as the Lord of the Sabbath, for he is the gentle master who provides rest for the souls of all who come to him. Yet the Pharisees, instead of coming to him, plot to kill him! They provide the precise example of what ought not be done. Jesus points out that the heart of their error stems from failing to live by Hosea 6:6. They do not acknowledge Jesus as God and they do not show mercy or compassion for people, but instead condemn the innocent. The finishing question pushes people to consider what it might mean for them to take to heart Hosea 6:6 in their treatment of others and their treatment of God (and therefore their response to Jesus).

1. 'Messiah' means 'anointed one'.

LEADER'S NOTES

8. JESUS: THE BIG BROTHER YOU WANT

Matthew 12:22-50

▶ **Remember: 60/40/20**

Getting started

As with many other passages in Matthew, 12:22-50 emphasizes the fact that how a person responds to Jesus is more important than what they might know, how important they might seem or who they are descended from. The 'Getting started' question has no hidden agenda; it is just meant to tease out circumstances in everyday life where *who* you know is more important than *what* you know.

Studying the passage

There is a great deal of information and detail in this passage. Except for the final section, where Jesus is informed that his family are wanting to speak to him (Matt 12:46-50), this passage is structured around the conflicts between Jesus and the Pharisees. Questions 1-2 are therefore intended as overview questions that require a quick re-read of the passage, observing its key details.

The passage tells us a great deal about Jesus. He is able to heal the demon-possessed and so, according to his own parable, is able to bind the strong man (Satan) and carry off his possessions. We have just been told that, in fulfilment of Isaiah 42:1-3, the Spirit of God is on Jesus (Matt 12:18-21). Therefore, he is driving out the demons by the Spirit of God. We also see that whoever is not with him is against him, and whoever does not gather with him scatters. Jesus regards those who are with him as being those who do the will of his Father in heaven, and he regards them as his family. He sees himself as greater than the prophet Jonah and greater than great and wise King Solomon.

Jesus knows what his enemies are thinking, and he knows how evil spirits and Satan operate. He also knows what people can and cannot be forgiven, and how people will be judged on the day of judgement.

While the Pharisees say very little compared to Jesus in this passage, what they do say (as well as what is said about them) reveals a great deal. Their verdict on Jesus is that he is only able to cast out demons because he is in league with the prince of demons—a verdict they come to when they hear that the people are beginning to wonder if Jesus is the Messiah. They appear in danger of committing the unforgivable sin, and Jesus describes them as being evil and a brood of vipers. They claim to want to see a miraculous sign from Jesus, but Jesus says this is simply an indication of their wickedness. He implies that unlike those who heard the preaching of Jonah, they have not repented at the preaching of one greater than Jonah. Unlike the Queen of Sheba, they have not listened to the one with great wisdom.

Jesus responds to the Pharisees' charge in three ways. First, he points out that a kingdom divided against itself cannot stand. Next, he points out that, according to the Pharisees' logic, others who drive out demons (whom the Pharisees approve of) must also be demonic (v. 27).[1] Third, Jesus argues that he is stronger than Satan, and that is why he can drive out demons. This is the meaning of the unusual parable Jesus tells about the strong man (v. 29). It is unusual, because Jesus compares himself to a robber! Similarly the strong man referred to is not Jesus (as people may initially think), but Satan. Jesus is the 'stronger man' who can bind Satan and so "plunder his house" of demon-possessed people. Question 4 attempts to mine this truth for its rich pastoral value. Many fear the activity of demons, but those who trust in Jesus can be reassured that their Lord is stronger than any evil spirit and so they have nothing to fear.

Jesus' reply to the Pharisees' accusation leads to him issuing a warning about the unforgivable sin. He states that while sins committed against the Son of Man can be forgiven, speaking against the Holy Spirit will not be forgiven, either in this age or the one to come. He goes on to warn that on the judgement day our words will either acquit or condemn us.

It seems that the Pharisees were at least *in danger* of committing the sin against the Holy Spirit. Obviously this cannot simply mean speaking against Jesus, for Jesus makes it plain that such speaking can be forgiven. Rather, it appears to be wilful and persistent rejection of the truth revealed by the Spirit, in full knowledge that this is what one is doing. The sin against the Holy Spirit, then, may be defined as knowing the testimony of the Spirit regarding Jesus, yet persistently rejecting it.

Understanding this section is important pastorally, as many people fear that they have committed the unforgivable sin, either because they regard certain sins as particularly heinous, or because they are anxious that they have vigorously opposed Jesus at times. Those who are anxious in these ways can be reassured that the way to avoid the unforgivable sin is to receive the Spirit's testimony about Jesus, that he is Christ the Lord.

The Pharisees further demonstrate their wickedness by asking Jesus for a sign. While their question may have a ring of piety to it, ultimately the request springs from unbelief. To begin with, Jesus has already healed a man with a withered hand and driven out demons in their presence. Matthew tells us that Jesus is unambiguously fulfilling prophecies in Isaiah with these types of signs. Yet the question also betrays unbelief, in that it assumes Jesus must fulfil their demands of him, rather than that they should obey his demand upon them to repent.

Jesus' words offer a stern warning of judgement to anyone today who might demand that God give them a sign before they will believe (question 9). It is evident from Jesus' answer that his death and resurrection is a sign—indeed *the* sign—that vindicates him.

The final verses of the passage deal with Jesus' response to an interjection—that his family is waiting for him. The assumption is that the desire of Jesus' biological family to have his attention ought to take priority over any activity that Jesus is engaged in. Jesus does not share that assumption. The reason he gives is that he *is* giving attention to his family—those who do the will of his Father in heaven.

Jesus' brief response also carries two significant pastoral challenges to those in your group. It is firstly a challenge to all who give biological family relationships a priority over the commands of Jesus and the demands of being in his spiritual family. In Jesus' mind, the bonds formed by his blood shed on the cross are thicker than those formed by biology; indeed, they constitute a Christian's true family bonds. The wonderful truth of this is that Christ is our brother and all who follow him are our family.

Jesus' response is also a challenge to any who give his mother, Mary, undue prominence. Jesus' response shows that he regards *any* believer as highly as he regards Mary; there can therefore be no grounds for giving her a special status. Since this is one of the passages in the Gospels which most clearly highlights the error of excessively exalting Mary, a question is included to draw this out.

To finish

While this passage is one that is largely structured around the conflict between Jesus and the Pharisees, it is also characterized by stern warnings. Jesus' warnings come in response to what the Pharisees say—it is their words that condemn them. The finishing question therefore focuses on the warning Jesus gives in verses 36-37, and encourages people to reflect carefully on what this might mean for their own speech. It is an encouragement to make sure that how we speak makes it clear that we acknowledge Jesus as the king of God's kingdom, and that we are part of his family.

1. Exactly what Jesus is referring to here is not clear from the text. Whilst not necessarily approving of these 'exorcists', Jesus seems to be speaking about their strange though not uncommon methods. But the argument Jesus makes is not affected by the specific methods involved.